Barely Still, Barely Stirring

poems by

James Green

Finishing Line Press
Georgetown, Kentucky

Barely Still, Barely Stirring

ACKNOWLEDGMENTS

The author gratefully acknowledges the publications in which the following poems first appeared:

Sunrise on Mt. Ranier, *Avocet*
A Few Minutes after Takeoff, *Poetic Hours*
Camping on a Mountain, *Poetic Hours*
Barely Still, Barely Stirring, *Hidden Oak*
Prairie Storm, *Revival*
The Visitor, *Reach of Song*
Digging a Foundation, *St. Linus Review*
The Adoption, *LILIPOH*

The author also wishes to acknowledge Poets and Patrons, Inc., of Chicago, for its recognition of "The Adoption" as First Honorable Mention in its 2018 competition.

Publisher: Leah Maines
Editor: Christen Kincaid
Cover Art: https://pxhere.com/en/photo/1332197, in the public domain
Author Photo: David Green
Cover Design: Elizabeth Maines McCleavy

Printed in the USA on acid-free paper.
Order online: www.finishinglinepress.com
                also available on amazon.com

Author inquiries and mail orders:
Finishing Line Press
P. O. Box 1626
Georgetown, Kentucky 40324
U. S. A.

Table of Contents

Barely Still, Barely Stirring 1

Fingernail of a Moon 2

Tears at the Edge of a Canyon 3

Blue Heron 4

Camping on a Mountain under a Comet 5

Ebbing Season 6

Summit Trail 7

Prairie Storm 8

August Nights 9

Sunrise on Mt. Rainer 10

The Visitor 11

Fog 12

Remembering the Occasion of Hiking at Midnight 13

Hearthfires 14

Summer Thunderstorm 15

Train from Ely to London 16

A Few Minutes after Takeoff from LAX 17

River's Grace 18

I Search for a Cassowary, Find Bats 19

Digging the Foundation for a House 20

The Adoption 21

The Bells of Armagh 23

Barely Still, Barely Stirring

Barely still barely stirring
my moment on the path is making
unfamiliar sound a rabbit dares.
In morning mist become of morning
a dove unseen affirms the warning,
barely still barely stirring.

Barely still barely stirring
the hedge rows in the mist dissolving
like the footpath where I run.
Past a rye grass pasture soaking
past a stream barely flowing
barely still barely stirring.

Barely still barely stirring
to churchyard ruins emerging
where an archway aligns the sun
now seeping through the dappled sky.
No longer running, I stand there listening.
Barely still. Barely stirring.

Fingernail of a Moon

In the prairie sky
the fingernail of a moon
presses a seam
in Cassiopeia's gown.

Nightscape rinses
the memory of daytime
and purple is the promise
of tomorrow's sunrise.

Tears at the Edge of a Canyon

As we sat on the stone
at the rim of the canyon
we listened to the river
and the echo of three white birds
soaring at eye level.
The only other sound
came from a tear,
honoring a friend.

Blue Heron

The beach was the fringe
of the city's lights,
an edge lighted by a lopsided moon.

Along the causeway headlights
shot converging beams of light
at the shadows

but we walked
where the night led us
and listened to the surf

on the other side of darkness
barely beyond the ebbing tide
when a blue heron appeared

etching itself on the horizon
like a signpost stuck
in the sandbar offshore.

The imperceptible distance
between us closed as gradually
as the city's glow rose into the sky

and the silhouette stretched,
its tapered beak like a needle
trying to peck a pinhole
in the veil draping the night.

Camping on a Mountain under a Comet

We chose a leeward campsite offering care
and made our preparations for the night;
a stone became a table to prepare
the ample meal we shared in hushed delight.

The mountain's shadow eased across the lake
as twilight rinsed the halo of the moon
ascending while a crimson sunset's wake
remembered the departed afternoon.

Cocooned inside our slumber-sacks for sleep,
surrendering to night against the chill,
we watched first stars in bloom begin to seep
inside and listened as the wind-song stilled.

Awakened by a hush I stepped outside
In time to see the comet's widening stream,
a spray of pulsing lights in nightscape's tide,
and wondered if I were inside a dream.

Ebbing Season

The ebbing season of the river's soul
surrounds a silhouette against the sky
while shadows wash upon the naked shoal
and yesterday awaits the night's good-bye.
Some driftwood tangled on the bank still clings
to seasons left from dreams afraid to wake;
a memory drifting in the river stings
a heart with nothing left but hope to break.
Whatever heaven hides behind the moon
still lingers like an echo from the night.
We do not know which dreams eclipsed will soon
become debris inside the river's flight.
Can hope endure another day's disuse
if night is running out of dreams to lose?

Summit Trail

Switchbacking in a forest of pines
the trail led us upward to a ridge
above the timberline crowning the valley

and we stopped to rest above the gray fold of smog
we could not see while in its midst, obscuring the day
of our origin like the cloud of unknowing.

At eye's level a deeper blue of sky expands,
and we float on the rising wave of mountains
stretching the dimensions of sight.

Prairie Storm

Yellows and grays commingle
on the horizon early in the evening.

An unsympathetic chill settles
on the backs of livestock, stirring.

Thunder gathers itself slowly,
like the growl deep in the throat of a dog.

This is when I measure the distance
with light and sound and time,

as though this knowledge matters
as though prediction alters outcome.

Rivulets on the ground form systems
and course into the creek that swells

until disappearing behind the steel gray
filaments of rain falling onto red clay.

Hail pellets drum roll across the porch roof,
bounce off the flatbed of the truck like spilled marbles,

plopping into blood brown puddles to melt layer
by occluded layer.

August Nights

On a hot August night I lay on a concrete slab porch
and let it soak up the heat while the stars fall around me
like snow and I wonder if I can count them.
How many nights would it take? Better to count the nights
than to try to count the stars. Stars and nights go uncounted
but August nights return.

In the bottom of the canoe I feel its ribs hold me steady
under the moving canopy of stars, while a trickle of lake water
runs down its keel, and cools my spine on a hot August night.
Dad's paddle slips soundlessly into the water,
and I watch through sleepy gauze a star stationed over our camp.
The night's catch thumps against the side, making the only noise.

Twilight is the best time to measure the stars,
I was taught by the navigator on an August night.
I found a suitable target in the western sky,
focused my sextant and turned the dial slowly,
the horizon rising to meet the star. Of course,
a good plot depends upon knowing the name of your star.

Countless stars still smother hot August nights.
From my mortgaged patio I looked for one, just one,
to fall into the canyon between the skies.
A star I cannot name from stars I cannot count
I balance on the tip of my finger, pointing as a bridge
disappearing into the hot August night.

Sunrise on Mt. Rainer

along ledges to darkness
no one knew how deep
stepping across crevasses
yawning in the night

my head lamp trained
a few steps ahead
where another climbs
in the rim of the light

toward a summit
no one can see

the climbing line
is my safety if I fall
or my peril
if he falls

stopping for nourishment
graduating layers of sunrise
become vestments for mass

and the sun like a sharp edge
slices away at the night
and the glacier
begins to glisten

The Visitor

The silence of the desert night turned wild,
wind slapped against the side of our tent,
the limber stays reversing bend and bow,
tie-downs humming like Aeolian harps.
We had chosen this site because of the mesa's cover
but the wind got up in the night, rounded the rock
outcroppings and came at us broadside
gust after gust with tactical precision.
I do not remember falling into sleep
or when the wind subsided in the night.
At morning, breaking camp we saw the tracks
where in the night a coyote had circled us
and, unperturbed by the vagaries of the wind
curled up on our leeward side to share our site.

Fog

Fog diffuses daylight
and this morning's fresh snow,
swallowing exactness.
A pond reflects the void
in the stillness of its surface.
Even sound is opaque.
Lingering behind, perhaps,
is the sun not yet decided.

Remembering the Occasion of Hiking at Midnight,
December 31, 1999, on a mountain trail
overlooking Palm Springs

We followed the trail in the dark,
climbing all the way into midnight
in the seam between the mountain top
and the city below, miniaturized,
its voice rising like a chorus
in some ancient amphitheater.

Satisfied by our progress into the wilderness,
we perched on a rock, straddling the moment,
faced the summit, and waited for silence.
But the city's celebration persisted,
following us into the quiet, so we turned around –
amplified bass and percussion throbbing
up canyon walls, colors exploding into the sky
below us, chasing after the darkness
only to fall as ashes onto the desert floor.

We sat in the seam between millennia
on the side of the mountain,
partly facing the city,
partly facing the stillness.

Hearthfires

A chilling wind collides against the flame
and numbs the warmth inside my hearth. Now fears
of night without a fire appear as tears,
forgeting fire soon spent. Now gone. Once tame.
I pray quiescent fire still banked unites
anew within my hearth, and breath provides
new life to waiting embers where resides
my hope a dancing flame again ignites.
But fire can rage inside, so bright the light
soon crazed, then gorged, last leaving night's desire
in frenzy. Worse are flames reluctant, fire
unwilling, while I shiver in the night.
A kinder fire within my hearth would keep
me warm against the night, and let me sleep.

Summer Thunderstorm

Convulsing lightning
the sky argues with itself,
gasps for a surge of breath,
heaving breath, then thunder
absorbed by time mumbles
like monotonous surf, and
pellets of rain as rivulets spread
on the ground like arteries and
course into systems of drainage.
The river swells, then disappears
behind a veil of rain, leaving
the black shinny mirror of last night
another memory.

Train from Ely to London

I saw my reflection in the window, like a ghost
haunting, superimposed on pastures of barley
rolling by to the rhythm of the train carriage rocking
and the rapid three count percussion from the rails.
At the top of the frame a cloud's feathered edge
diffused the sun and an array of sunbeams,
variegated hedges and daisies generously scattered,
when a shot of sunlight ricocheted off a tiny crystal
imbedded in a stone in a loose-stack fence,
seizing the horizon in a blinding instant,
and the scene entered the present and proximate
when the reflection disappeared and my face
holographic turned to the conductor
collecting the fare.

A Few Minutes after Takeoff from LAX

In the aperture of my window
a single cloud points the way
into the ambiguous horizon
and the surf with feathered edges
stands still.

Banking away from the sun
bearings are bewildered
in the absence of landscape
and miles begin to grow
as long as time.

River's Grace

As light as a leaf
on top of the water
I glide from the bank
into the channel and

with a single stroke, deep,
with a twist at the end,
I turn the bow, letting it
slide with the current.

An occasional nudge
of my paddle silently
keeps me to the center
inside the river's grace.

I Search for a Cassowary, Find Bats

The sign indicated cassowary crossing
and so we kept a keen eye out for one, trusting
the credibility of a South Queensland highway worker,
parked our car on the side of road and quietly
began to stalk the quarry, camera in hand,
remembering the ranger's warning:
Never look a cassowary in the eye.
Enrages them, he added, raising his brow to make the point.
I slipped the camera back into my pants pocket,
scanning the shadows on the forest floor
for the man-sized bird with claws like cargo hooks
harmless unless riled, who hunts seeds to transplant.
We all have our jobs to do, I thought, the strange bird
who replenishes the rainforest with his seed-rich feces,
the ranger who knows these things, the road worker
and his sign, and mine too, I suppose, although
it is not nearly so efficient as the cassowary's.
The ranger was right about eye contact, too.
Once I did lock stares with one, in a zoo
before I heard about this aversion to intimacy.
The frenzied bird rammed its beak into the chain link,
hissed and spewed an anger too horrible for instinct,
the madness in its pupils too concentrated for mere
territorial assertion—this was that other kind of look and
noise from within that we do not understand, only fear.
Such is the nature of knowledge, an incident here or there,
an explanation someplace without context then patched
together on the edge of a forest but not until it has some use.
I never saw a cassowary in the forest that day, despite the sign
that encouraged me in estimating my prospects. Although,
I spied some bats, hundreds of them actually, drip-drying themselves
of sunlight filtering through the tree-tops, an anteater nosing
about a tangle roots, and a bird with translucent blue tail-feathers
whose perch was near the colony of bats.

Digging the Foundation of the House,
Near Santiago Atitlan, Guatemala

Dig here, Miguel said. He spoke solemnly,
this wide and this deep, true, with smooth sides,
pointing to the space between the lines he
made with lime on the black sandy soil.

He began, each arc of his pick exact.
Excavation for a house is easy
if there are no boundaries or angry rocks
or roots, sinewy roots embedded like

systems of live tendrils. Miguel gave me
his pick, handle hand fashioned, and a worn
flat blade shovel for scooping up progress.
This wide and this deep, he reminded me.
True, with smooth sides.

Self-willed rocks deflected each plunge
of my pick answered every strike
resolutely until hand dug then pried
from the bulwarks. Miguel still insisted,

foundations must begin with a clean trench.
The choicest stones we saved for the footings,
chosen for their size and shape and hardness.
Miguel knew which ones and the rest we heaved

aside with the tangled roots we chopped to death
with machetes, leaving them like bones to dry.
Foundations must begin with a clean trench:
this wide and this deep, true, with smooth sides.

The Adoption, Near Ukarumpa, Papua New Guinea

The scent of green firewood rises from the village invisible in haze
as we pick our way down the footpath, the red clay steps glistening.

Children appear out of the mist to be first to see the miracle,
to be first to see the story their mothers tell.

At a clearing in the village all crane their necks for a look at the tiny
     face
scrunching in search of a nipple, lips smacking to form a perfect seal.

An elder holds the baby aloft, processes to where the child was born,
to where the child's father prepares the feast to celebrate the adoption.

Sobs from the fringe, hushed the way we try to hide half-buried grief,
tell of other faces whose clefts were not re-sculpted and who starved.

A mother is consoled by one whose own tears are stifled by time;
such is the nature of miracles and such is the nature of grief absent of
     miracles.

At the edge each tastes the salt of her tears, suffering proof of hope,
suffering a feast that celebrates the succor of life.

Young women nurse their babies, their men gather scrapes of firewood,
and old women with yellow teeth chatter and stare at the *whiteskins*.

One offers to share her space under the eve of a bamboo hut
where she waits out a shower. Courtesy runs deep in her eyes.

In a pit coals glow in their ashes where tubers rolled in banana leaves
roast beneath a spit of green wood, turning chickens. Smoke rises into
     haze.

After the last course men light pipes, women collect their children,
and all edge toward the father who is first to speak.

He begins his story solemnly, and since the importance of a feast
is gauged by the number who tell stories, more follow.

The *whiteskin* man waits his turn, then speaks in their language,
as he is *wun tok* and has told them stories before, also about miracles.

A grandfather speaks, then a man who furrows his brow the way one
reserves for matters of consequence, as the issue was adoption.

He speaks of fate, of the future of their village, and why their voice
must be as *wun bel*. The speeches end. The father nods consent

and with eyes that speak the mother gives away the baby
nursing loudly from a plastic bottle cradled by the *whiteskin* woman.

On the way up the mountain rain begins to sting and blood red rivulets
    trickle
down the path. The new mother clutches her baby, concentrating on
    each step.

A barefoot girl races to meet the new mother, reaches for the baby, cradles
    him with
one slender arm and balancing with the other like an aerial artist springs
    ahead.

At the top, beside a jeep parked on the side of a rutted road,
she waits, swaying, rearranging the baby's swaddling.

The Bells of Armagh:
*A True Account of an Afternoon at St. Patrick's Cathedral
in Armagh, June 22, 1998, as Remembered by Two Tourists*

As you
knelt in prayer,
I rose to light candles,
noticing the organist practicing
and the sunlight streaming
through the rosette.

Elfish and indelibly signed
by the artist in him,
he interrupted my prayer
to show me his church.
Each relief, each window
was a special intention.
Playfully, like the light
in the arches above us,
he raised the corner of the rug
in front of the altar to reveal
the guild, remembering the weavers
on the day of presentation and smiled
and begged his pardon to leave,
illusively as he came.

I lighted my candles and turned.
How did I know he would find you also?
Then I remembered: You both pray in music.
And he invited you then me
into his bell tower as he already
knew somehow we were companions.

Opening a weathered door
he led us into an inner chamber:
to the spiral staircase
to the loft
past another door
to another spiral,

which, he delighted in telling us,
was past the point
where we were insured,
where the birds silent and stiff
had come to die.

In the tower he eased himself
onto his bench at an ancient keyboard
to make his music,
and you climbed the ladder, higher,
to the belfry, to await his song.

"For St. Patrick," he said,
with the excitement of a little boy
about to play at his first recital.

Massive waves of music
oceans of music
flooded the belfry
spilled over the valley
into the infinite melody
he performed from a keyboard
connected to systems of levers,
pulleys, and cords,
and once silent bells.

After the music of the bells,
I climbed the ladder
where you stood
still,
flattened against the wall
and I listened again in your eyes
and silence was never the same.

Jim has worked as a naval officer, deputy sheriff, high school English teacher, professor of education, and administrator in both public schools and universities. Recipient of two Fulbright specialist grants, he has served as a visiting scholar at the University of Limerick in Ireland and at the National Chung Cheng University in Taiwan. His academic publications include three books, as well as numerous articles in professional journals. His poetry has appeared in literary magazines in England, Ireland, and the USA; and published collections include *Stations of the Cross* (Finishing Line Press, 2008) and *The Color of Prayer: Poems on Rembrandt Painting the Bible* (Shanti Arts Publishing, 2019).

He received B.A. and M.S. degrees in English and education from Missouri State University, a Ph.D. in education from Saint Louis University, and an M.F.A. in creative writing from Antioch University Los Angeles.

www.ingramcontent.com/pod-product-compliance
Lightning Source LLC
LaVergne TN
LVHW021127080426
835510LV00021B/3345